HOW TO BECOME AN ENTREPRENEUR

About the Author

Hey guys,

I am OX, aka iFadedHer. I am a 22-year-old barber who lives in Charlotte, NC. The reason why I decided to write this book was so that people could start following their dreams. I am tired of people depending on a paycheck when you should start depending on yourself.

This book is going to lead you step by step on how to LIVE YOUR BEST LIFE. I hope you enjoy it and you start following your dreams.

Follow my IG: iFadedHer

How to Become an Entrepreneur

Copyright © 2020 by Ox of iFadedHer

Editing and Formatting: Jessann Hahner

Kansas City, Missouri

All rights reserved. No part of this publication may be reproduced, distributed, or transmitted in any form or by any means, including photocopying, recording, or other electronic or mechanical methods, without the prior written permission of the publisher, except in the case of brief quotations embodied in critical reviews and specific other noncommercial uses permitted by copyright law.

HOW TO BECOME AN ENTREPRENEUR

Contents

Introduction 5

Chapter 1 – Find Your Passion 7

    Service Businesses 7

    Product Businesses 8

Chapter 2 – Training and Education 9

    Evaluate Training Programs Before Investing Time and Money in Them 9

    Free Courses 10

Chapter 3 – Create a Business Plan 11

    Pick a Format for your Business Plan 11

        Traditional Business Plans 11

        Lean Startup Business Plans 14

Chapter 4 - Fund Your New Business 17

    1. Think about Factoring 17

    2. Get a Traditional Business Bank Loan 17

    3. Utilize a Charge Card 18

    4. Start Tapping Your 401k 18

    5. Crowdfunding 18

    6. Pursue Angel Investors 19

    8. Get an SBA Loan 19

    9. Ask Friends and Family 20

HOW TO BECOME AN ENTREPRENEUR

10. Try a Microloan 21

Chapter 5 – Determine Your Ideal Customer and Target Audience 22

Chapter 6 – Create a Website 25

    Steps to Creating a Website 26

    Get Content for your Site 26

Chapter 7 – Start Networking 27

    In-Person Networking 27

    Social Networking 30

    Facebook 31

    Instagram 31

    LinkedIn 32

    Pinterest 32

    Twitter 32

    YouTube 32

    Quora 33

    Imgur 33

Chapter 8 – Market Your Business 34

    Brand Awareness 34

    Promote a New Product or Service 35

    Gather Customer Feedback 35

    Boost User Engagement 35

- Set Clear Goals 36
- Determine How You Will Reach your Audience 36
  - Measuring Marketing Campaigns 38
- Chapter 9 – Do you need to Incorporate or Become an LLC? 40
  - What is an LLC? 40
  - What is an S Corp vs. a C Corp? 40
  - What is a Sole Proprietorship? 41
  - Which one is right for your business? 41
- Chapter 10 – Grow Your Team 42
- Chapter 11 – Keeping Your Finances in Line 44
- Chapter 12 – Never Stop Learning and Improving your Business 47
- Disclaimer 48
- References 49

Introduction

All too often, young bright and talented people end up trudging away at jobs that make them miserable instead of following their dreams of becoming an entrepreneur. Whether this is due to a lack of information, motivation, or the right tools, we aim to fix that and take you from aspiring to be an entrepreneur to thriving as a successful entrepreneur. While no two journeys will ever be the same, consider this your guidebook to get you out of the learning loop and into taking actionable steps toward your success.

The most important takeaway you can get from this book is to start. Take the first step, three more, and keep pushing forward toward your dream each day. Your biggest enemy in starting your business will be yourself, stop pushing things off for another day, and start taking action.

"*You can do whatever you set your mind to if you just roll up your sleeves, get in there, and do it.*"

- **Marie Forleo**, Everything is Figureoutable: How One Simple Belief Can Help Us Overcome Any Obstacle and Create Unstoppable Success (Forleo 2019)

Marie Forleo set the stage in 2019 and showed young women and men around the world that you don't have to know the answer to everything when you're starting out, but that you can figure it out as you go. She forged her way forward, and we urge you to follow in her footsteps and start your own business. Having a dream is great, but without action, that is all it will ever be.

So many people have led the way before you, yet your business will be unique because it has something no other firm has, you. You are the critical factor that makes your business different.

Whether your business succeeds or fails depends on the steps you take and what you bring to the table. Greet each day with a growth mindset and set off for an adventure in entrepreneurism.

"Here's to the crazy ones. The misfits. The rebels. The troublemakers. The round pegs in the square holes. The ones who see things differently. They are not fond of rules. And they have no respect for the status quo. You can quote them, disagree with them, glorify or vilify them. About the only thing you cannot do is ignore them. Because they change things, they push the human race forward. And while some may see them as the crazy ones, we see genius. Because the people who are crazy enough to think they can change the world, are the ones who do."

― Russell Brunson, Expert Secrets: The Underground Playbook for Finding Your Message, Building a Tribe, and Changing the World (Brunson 2017)

Chapter 1 – Find Your Passion

The step that often takes entrepreneurs the longest is finding your passion, and deciding what your business venture should be. Take a look inward, and find out what speaks to you. The good news is, you can do what you love and get paid for it. The bad news is, it will take hard work and determination to go from a passionate idea to a profitable business.

First, decide if your new business will provide a service or a product. While some services can be productized and sold as packages, fulfilling the services will take a lot of time out of your day. Pick a product or service that speaks to your heart, one that you will not mind fulfilling day after day.

Make a list of things you love, a list of things that make money, and figure out what falls into both categories.

As a service business, you can also offer products. Think of a hairstylist; they offer hair care services, but also offer salon-quality products in most instances.

Service Businesses

Service businesses provide intangible work products such as business consultation, writing, cleaning, insurance, and even transportation. (Business Dictionary n.d.)

When selling services, you will be selling your own expertise and showing how your services can improve the lives of business owners or consumers. Depending on the services you offer, you will either need business to business marketing, or business to consumer marketing plans.

Product Businesses

Product businesses provide a tangible product to consumers or other businesses. These can be any type of product you can imagine. (Business Dictionary n.d.)

When selling products, you want to highlight the features of the product and how they fit your ideal customer's needs.

Chapter 2 – Training and Education

You do not have to hold any particular degrees to start your own business, but you should determine what training and education are appropriate for your specific business venture. Reading this book is a step in the right direction for training and education toward becoming an entrepreneur. Look at the specialized skills that will make you more successful. An investment in education and training that makes your company more successful is imperative to create a thriving business.

Consider learning things like:

- SEO
- Copywriting;
- Writing business plans;
- Obtaining investors;
- Specialized skills for your business;
- Closing sales;
- Managing employees;
- Social media growth;
- Marketing plans and;
- So much more.

Evaluate Training Programs Before Investing Time and Money in Them

Not all courses are created equal, do not get swindled out of thousands of dollars for a course that will not get you the results you are seeking. While the most crucial factor in whether a course will work for you or not is your dedication to taking action, be vigilant in vetting your courses before committing.

Check testimonials, ask for results from previous participants in the course, and verify that these are real people. The last thing you want is to get scammed when you are just starting down your path of creating your own business. While training is a valuable investment, just like any investment, you need to do your research before you hand over your hard-earned cash.

Free Courses

While not all free courses are worth your time, there is a lot of value in free courses online. You can learn everything from the specific steps to form an LLC, to how to close sales for your business. Look at free offers from course creators and start collecting their freebies that resonate with your business to build your knowledge base. Trying out a course creator's free offers is a great way to see if their paid training or coaching programs are a good fit for you without spending money on their courses and then hoping for the best. Treat free courses the same as you would a paid course, and pull every ounce of value you can from free information.

Chapter 3 – Create a Business Plan

Your business plan is the solid foundation from which you will build your entrepreneurial empire. Write your business plan out with clear goals in mind, and follow these steps to make sure you have everything you need. The first step when writing your business plan is choosing the format, then building from there. You can start with a template by searching the web to make things as painless as possible, or write your own from scratch.

Pick a Format for your Business Plan

There is no cookie-cutter solution to writing your business plan, each business is unique, and their business plans should be as well. As long as your plan meets your business's needs, you're doing it right. The majority of business plans can be described as either traditional or lean startups.

Traditional plans are the most common, but they require more upfront work and are often over twenty pages.

Lean startup business plans are seen less often, but have gained popularity in recent years. A lean plan summarizes key points of your plan, and can often be accomplished in a day. (My Biz Starts Here n.d.)

Traditional Business Plans

If you are detail-oriented and want every facet of your business included in your plan, you may prefer a traditional business plan.

There are no hard and fast rules that say you have to stick to the outline precisely. Use what your business needs. A traditional business plan uses a combination of the following nine sections.

1. Executive summary

Quickly state to what your organization is and why it will be fruitful. Incorporate your mission statement, fundamental data about your organization's authority group, representatives, area, and your product or service. You ought to incorporate financial data and significant development plans if you intend to request financing.

2. Company description

Utilize your company description portrayal to give specific data about your organization. Expound on the issues your business settles. Be explicit, and rattle off the customers, association, or organizations your organization intends to serve.

Clarify the upper hands that will make your business a triumph. Are there specialists in your group? Have you discovered the ideal area for your store? Your organization's company description is the spot to brag about your qualities and strengths.

3. Market analysis

You will require a decent comprehension of your industry standpoint and ideal clients or customers. Serious exploration of competitors will give you what different organizations are doing and what the qualities they possess. When conducting your market research, search for patterns and themes. Answer these questions:

- What do fruitful contenders do?
- Why do their strategies work?
- What would you be able to improve?

4. Organization and management

Explain how your business will be organized and who will run it.

Depict the legal structure of your business. State whether you will incorporate your business as an S Corporation, C Corporation, are forming a general limited partnership, are an LLC, or you will be a sole proprietor.

Utilize a hierarchical outline to lay who is accountable for what in your organization. Show how every individual's interesting experience will add to the achievement of your endeavor. Consider including resumes and CVs of key colleagues.

5. Service or product line

Portray what you sell or what services you offer. Clarify how it benefits your clients and what the product lifecycle resembles. Offer your arrangements for protected intellectual property, such as copyright or patent filings. Include any research and development you have done for your product or service.

6. Marketing and sales

There is no single method to move toward an advertising technique. Your system ought to develop and change to accommodate your extraordinary needs.

Your objective in this area is to portray how you will pull in and hold clients. You will additionally depict how a deal will occur. You will allude to this segment later when you make budgetary projections, so try to portray your total altogether promoting and deals techniques.

7. Funding request

In case you are requesting financing, this is the place you will plot your subsidizing prerequisites. You will likely obviously clarify how much subsidizing you will require throughout the following five years and where you will spend the funding.

Indicate whether you prefer equity or debt, the terms you would like applied, and the period your solicitation will cover. Give a definite depiction of how you will utilize your assets. Determine if you need assets to purchase hardware or materials, pay rates, or spread explicit bills until income increments. Continuously incorporate a depiction of your future essential monetary plans, such as taking care of obligation or selling your business.

8. Financial projections

Supplement your request for funding with money related projections. You want to persuade potential investors that your business is steady and will be fruitful.

If you have the information, incorporate salary explanations, accounting reports, and income proclamations for the last three to five years. On the off chance that you have other security, you could set against an advance, make a point to show it now.

Give a forthcoming monetary standpoint to the following five years. Incorporate estimated salary articulations, asset reports, income proclamations, and capital consumption financial plans. For the primary year, be considerably increasingly explicit and utilize quarterly — or even month to month — projections. Make a point to clarify your projections unmistakably, and match them to your subsidizing demands.

This is an excellent spot to utilize diagrams and graphs to recount to the monetary story of your business.

9. Appendix

Your appendix should include documents and supporting materials. Some things you may consider adding to the appendix of a traditional business plan:

- Credit history;
- Resumes;
- Photos of products;
- Reference letters;
- Permits and licenses;
- Patents and;
- Any other contracts.

Lean Startup Business Plans

You may favor a lean startup business plan format when you need to clarify or begin your business rapidly, your business is generally straightforward, or you plan to change and refine your strategy frequently.

Lean startup plans are typically visual and cover elements such as infrastructure, your value proposition, target customers, and finances.

These are the nine components of a Lean Startup Plan

Key Partners

Note different organizations or administrations you will work with to maintain your business. Consider providers, makers, subcontractors, and vital comparative partners.

Key Activities

Rundown the manners in which your business will increase revenue. Feature things like offering direct to shoppers, or utilizing innovation to take advantage of the sharing economy.

Key Resources

Rundown any asset you will use to make an incentive for your client. Your most significant resources could incorporate staff, capital, or licensed innovation. Remember to use business assets that may be accessible to ladies, veterans, Native Americans, and HUBZone organizations.

Value Proposition

Make an understood and convincing proclamation about the novel worth your organization brings to the market.

Customer Relationships

Depict how clients will interact with your business. Is it mechanized or individual? Face to face or on the web? Thoroughly consider the client experience through and through.

Customer Segments

Be explicit when you name your objective market. Your business will not be for everyone, so it is essential to have a depiction of who your business will serve.

Channels

Rundown the most significant ways you will converse with your clients. Most organizations utilize a blend of channels and enhance them after some time.

Cost structure

Will your organization center around diminishing costs or boosting value? Characterize your methodology. At that point, list the most critical prices you will confront seeking after it.

Streams of Revenue

Clarify how your organization will bring in cash. A few models are immediate deals, enrollment charges, and selling publicizing space. If your organization has various income streams, show them all.

Chapter 4 - Fund Your New Business

Big ideas often require big money, but that does not mean you have to fund your business on your own.

Discovering financing in any monetary climate can be daunting, regardless of whether you are searching for fire up reserves, cash-flow to extend, or cash to hang on through the difficult stretches. Yet, given our present status of undertakings, making sure about assets is as intense as could be. To assist you with finding the cash you need, check out these financing strategies, and what you should know while seeking them.

1. Think about Factoring

Factoring is an account strategy where an organization offers its receivables at a discounted rate to get money in advance. Organizations with helpless credit regularly utilize it. Notwithstanding, it is a costly method to raise reserves. If you pay a 2 percent charge to get funds 30 days ahead of time, it is proportional to a yearly loan fee of around 24 percent.

The monetary downturn has constrained organizations to look to elective financing techniques, and organizations are attempting to make factoring progressively safer. The trade permits organizations to offer their receivables to many organizations without a moment's delay, alongside flexible investments, banks, and other fund organizations. These loan specialists will provide on the solicitations, which can be sold in a group or each in turn.

2. Get a Traditional Business Bank Loan

Loaning principles have gotten a lot stricter. Yet banks like, J.P. Morgan Chase and Bank of America, have reserved surplus assets for independent company loaning. In today's economy, banks want to support small businesses, and the new standards are helping get more startups funded through traditional bank loans.

3. Utilize a Charge Card

Utilizing a charge card to subsidize your business can be risky. Fall behind on your installment, and your FICO score falls victim. Pay only the base every month, and you could create debt you will never escape. Be that as it may, utilized dependably, a charge card can stretch your business budget and keep you from running into cash flow issues in emergencies.

4. Start Tapping Your 401k

In case you are jobless and considering going into business, those assets you have aggregated in your 401(k) throughout the years can look quite enticing. What is more, because of arrangements in the assessment code, you really can take advantage of them without when you follow the correct advances. The means are sufficiently straightforward, however legitimately mind-boggling. You will need somebody with experience setting up a C company, and the fitting retirement plans to fold your retirement resources into your new business. Keep in mind that you are contributing your retirement reserves, which implies if things do not work out, you will also lose your savings.

5. Crowdfunding

A crowdfunding site can be a fun and successful approach to fund-raise for a moderately minimal effort, innovative project. You will set an objective for how cash you need to raise over a defined time frame, say, $2,000 over 45 days.

Pledgers give cash that goes toward your crowdfunded amount. This is not a strategy for long-haul funding, but can get a project off the ground quickly.

For the most part, venture makers offer motivators for pledging. There are prizes for different levels of monetary pledges.

6. Pursue Angel Investors
When pitching an angel financial specialist, all the old guidelines apply: be brief, avoid technical language, have an exit strategy in place. Be that as it may, the financial disturbance of the most recent couple of years has made a convoluted game considerably trickier.

Try not to be a crazed devotee: Did you start your organization since you are genuinely energetic about your thought or because you need to take advantage of the most recent pattern? Angel investors can detect the distinction and will not focus on those whose organizations are easy money scams.

Know your stuff: You'll need to advertise evaluations, serious examination, and strong showcasing and deals plans on the off chance that you hope to go anyplace with a heavenly attendant. Indeed, even youthful organizations need to show specialist information available they are going to enter just as the order to finish their blueprint.

Stay in contact: An angel investor may not be keen on your business immediately, particularly if you don't have a reputation as a fruitful business person. To battle that, you ought to detail an approach to keep them on top of it on vast turns of events, similar to a significant deal.

8. Get an SBA Loan
With banks hesitant to take any risks with their cash in the wake of the credit emergency, advances ensured by the U.S. Independent company Administration have become a hot product. Undoubtedly, assets to help exceptional breaks on expenses and assurances on SBA-upheld

credits have run out on various occasions. And keeping in mind that SBA-supported loans are available to any independent company, there are multiple capabilities, including:

Under the law, the SBA cannot ensure credits to organizations that can acquire the cash they need without a loan. So you need to apply for credit from a bank or other monetary organization and be turned down before getting an SBA loan.

To qualify as a private venture, your firm needs to meet the administration's meaning of an independent company for your industry.

Your business may need to meet other rules relying upon the sort of loan.

In the wake of discovering that your business meets the capabilities, you have to apply for a business credit from a money related organization that forms SBA advances since the SBA doesn't give direct loans. The bank's capabilities can be increasingly more rigid than the SBA.

9. Ask Friends and Family

Hitting up loved ones is the most widely recognized approach to back new businesses. When you transform friends and family into loan bosses, you are taking a chance with their money related future and endangering significant friendships and relationships. A great misstep is moving toward loved ones before a conventional field-tested strategy is even set up.

Supply formal budgetary projections, such as a proof-based appraisal of when your friends and family will see their cash once more. This proof ought to decrease the probability of undesirable shocks. It additionally tells your financial specialists you pay attention to their cash. It would be best if you likewise considered how the course of action will be organized. Is it accurate to say that you are offering value? Or then again, will this be a credit? Maybe, in particular, you have to underline the risk in question. Offer up a solid marketable strategy, yet remind them there is a decent possibility their cash will be lost. It is smarter to approach that forthright to Aunt Gladys instead of over Thanksgiving supper.

10. Try a Microloan

Barring collateral, credit history, and the ability to secure a traditional loan does not mean you are out of luck when it comes to getting a loan.

One choice is to apply for a microloan, a private company advance going from $500 to $35,000. Microloans are regularly so little that business banks cannot be tried loaning the assets. Rather than a bank, you have to go to a microlender.

Microloan companies are businesses that work uniquely in contrast to banks. Microlenders offer littler credit sizes, as a rule, require less documentation than banks, and frequently apply increasingly adaptable guaranteeing rules. There are two or three hundred microlenders all through the U.S. furthermore. They commonly charge marginally higher financing costs for advances than banks.

Chapter 5 – Determine Your Ideal Customer and Target Audience

Without knowing both who your target audience is and where they hang out, your advertising and marketing campaigns will fall flat. The last thing you want is to invest all of your hard work and time into creating the perfect company, only for it to fail because you weren't clear on who you serve. Marketing that targets a general audience is the least effective, so this will help you form an avatar of your perfect customer so you can better serve them, and better sell to them in turn.

Ask yourself, who do you actually want to work with, or, who do feel a strong pull to serve. Look at your product and service and ask who would have problems that your company can solve.

- What do these people look like?
- What type of jobs do they have?
- Where do they have dinner?
- Are they religious?
- What shows do they watch?
- What books do they read?
- What radio stations do they listen to?
- What brands are they already loyal to?
- Do they have children?
- What ideals do they hold above all else?

I know it sounds smart to start your business and serve every person, or cast a wide net with your marketing. The problem is, the wider your net when it comes to attracting customers, the bigger the holes in your marketing plan. Once you pin down who you want to attract, you can pin down the formula to attract them to your business.

The way you align with your audience and target them with your campaigns will be the determiner of how successful your business is. It is best to start with a writing exercise in character development. Create a profile or "avatar" of your customer and put it down on paper. In some cases, even draw a sketch of what your ideal customer looks like. The more detailed you get in your customer avatar, the better you can connect with them and find these customers online and in other formats with your marketing.

Once you know who your target audience is, you can start mapping out their pain points and start connecting those points to how your business can solve these issues. Ask questions that get to the heart of their issues. There are a few ways you can get the answers to the question: "What are my target customer's pain points that my product or service can solve?"

- Create targeted surveys with detailed questions that you can analyze.
- Research your competitors and evaluate their FAQ pages. In the FAQ sections, you will see questions their customers ask often, and can then use those questions and answers to dissect common pain points of customers who are already interested in what your business offers.
- Check out any reviews you or your competitors have online to pinpoint customer grievances, come up with better solutions based on this information.

Now that you know your ideal customer and what their pain points are, it is time to start solving their problems. Create unique solutions that appeal to the demographic you have chosen to target. Your marketing plan will evolve based on the stage your customers are in at the time. First, you will want to make them aware of your solutions and your brand, then get them to consider purchasing from you, then help them understand that your business has the best solutions to their problems. In every stage, you will want to show how your product or service improves the lives of those you choose to serve.

Your ability to pinpoint your target audience and serve them in with the best solutions will make or break your business. Do not be afraid of refining your plan when you see new pain points arise. Put yourself in your customer's shoes each time you add a new product or service to your business. Ask yourself, "Does this new idea solve an issue for my ideal customer? Is this a better solution than what is currently offered? How can we highlight the benefits of this product in a way that my ideal customer will respond to positively?"

Chapter 6 – Create a Website

In order to establish your business presence online, you will need to start with a website. Gone are the days when you would pay a webmaster thousands of dollars and wait months on end to get a "meh" website. In today's world, you can set up a website that is unique to your business with just a few clicks.

The most important factor in creating your website is driving traffic to your site. The number one way people will find your site online is through search engines like Google. In order to rank on Google as a local business, you will need to complete a Google My Business profile. Google My Business is a free service, and filling out the profile literally puts you on the map, Google Maps directory that is. Without this section, if people search for a "nail stylist near me," and you are a nail stylist who is not listed, you will not show up in the results.

When picking a theme and creating content for your site, keep your ideal customer in mind. What would they want to get out of your website? Are you answering all of their questions? Is your website easy to navigate? Make the user experience a priority to get people to shop with your company online and build brand authority.

Add a blog to your site to increase your search engine optimization. Create articles centered around your customer's pain points, targeting keywords that they are searching to find answers to their problems. Be the solution they are looking for when they need it the most.

Make sure you add an FAQ section and contact details to your site. Make it as easy as possible for your visitors to find what they need, and to contact you for more information.

If you are creating an online web store, make sure you set up a payment portal to accept multiple types of payments.

Steps to Creating a Website

1. Choose a web host
2. Choose a platform
3. Pick a domain name (stay close to your business name)
4. Install WordPress
5. Pick a Theme
6. Install SEO Plugins
7. Upload Content
8. Create an FAQ
9. Create a Contact Page
10. Create a Blog and schedule posts

Get Content for your Site

Your website needs fresh content in order to stay relevant to Google's search engines. Create new content for your site that is relevant to your business. If you serve customers locally, add local town and neighborhood names to your content. If you do not have time to create new content, you can purchase from freelancers or look into content mills for your article and blog post needs.

Chapter 7 – Start Networking

Establishing connections with other business owners is critical to growing your business and achieving success. Business owners can gain important industry knowledge and open new doors by networking. Sharing information and providing value to others is vital to staying relevant and building a successful business. If you have heard the phrase, "It's not what you know, it's who you know," and scoffed at the idea, then I have news for you. It is absolutely true. You can be the smartest businessperson in the world, but without the right connections, you will not secure investors, business partners, or gain trust in your industry.

In-Person Networking

Find local events for networking. Check out your local chamber of commerce for information on events, and attend chamber of commerce meetings to start meeting local business owners. To expand your reach with events, check out Eventbrite, and even Facebook Events for niche-specific networking events local to you. If you want to cast a wider net, look at surrounding areas or check out conferences that include members from all over the country, or even all over the world.

When you go to a networking event, people expect you to engage with others and well, network. I know this seems obvious, but I cannot tell you how many new business owners will show up to an event and close themselves off in a corner. In-person networking events are powerful tools to drive your business forward, but only if you interact with others and make a point to be seen.

Here are some tips to make the most out of in-person networking events.

Remember why you are there, and focus on creating relationships, not closing sales.

Like I stated above, everyone at these events is there for the purpose of networking. It may feel awkward to start a conversation with someone, but they are more like you than you might think. No one's first networking event is all smooth sailing, but the worst mistake you can make is becoming a wallflower.

Make it a point to spend limited time with each group, and have an exit strategy. Make sure you bring business cards to hand out, as people will be meeting with a wide range of other people, and they need a way to remember you.

Approach groups of people, and introduce yourself

At networking events, people tend to congregate in groups. If you are not already in one of those groups, it can feel near impossible to join one. You are going to have to interrupt people, but do so politely. Walk up, stand with the group, and say, "Excuse me, I am (your name) and I (what you do)." Then, tell whoever was talking to continue.

People will not stop talking at these events, so the only way to get into the inner circles is to force your way. Once you have entered a circle, make sure you are listening and gathering information about those around you to see who you want to add to your networking tribe.

Engage in Conversations and be Genuine

Listen first, then talk. Do not spend your time waiting to say something, instead respond to what others are saying. When you mirror others and show them you care about what they are saying, they are more responsive to creating business relationships and networking with you.

Ask questions that engage the people around you. The best questions are the ones that keep people talking. Instead of simply asking, "What does your company do?" Ask, instead, "Why are you passionate about your company?" Not all conversation has to be about business, either.

Ask people about their hobbies and find common ground. You might get more than solid business relationships. You could leave with a new gym partner, a new playdate partner for your children, or even a life-long friendship. Talk about what makes you unique, and create relationships with people who hold your values.

Have your elevator pitch ready when people do ask about your business, but do not spend all your time pitching at networking events.

Gather Contact Details and Excuse Yourself

Ask for contact details from people you want to create a deeper relationship with. Do not simply hand over your business card and leave it up to other people to find you. The success of building a larger network relies on you doing the follow-up, rather than relying on others to reach out to you. Of course, you should still hand over your business card, but make sure you get their information, as well.

Once you have collected contact details and made an impression, excuse yourself from the conversation and move on to another group. Cast a wide net at networking events. It may be more comfortable to stick with the same group of people, but this is only hurting your efforts and wasting your time. Especially if you have to pay to attend the event, the more people you talk to, the better your return on investment in networking.

Follow up After the Event ASAP

So the event ends, and you go home and set the business cards and contact information you've collected off to the side to follow up at a later date. Maybe you think you should wait a week before you reach out, so you do not look desperate. Do not wait. Follow up immediately.

Reach out while your conversations are still fresh in your mind, when you can still reference what you have talked about previously. Waiting to follow up loses your opportunities. The real power of networking is not what happens while you are at the event, but about how you foster relationships long-term.

Social Networking

Networking on social media is one of the fastest-growing trends in the business world. It is hard to believe it was not until 1997 that 50 million users in the United States gained access to the internet. Many young entrepreneurs were not even born when the big internet boom hit. The good news is, since young entrepreneurs have never known a time without the internet and social media, it is easy to jump in and start learning how to use these systems to grow your business.

Today, over a billion people are active on Facebook, out of 7.6 billion people on earth. There is no better way to connect with your audience than through social media that they use every day. If you have to choose only one social media network to focus your business efforts, Facebook is a clear choice. That is not to say there are no other social media sites that provide high value to your business and networking efforts. Let us take a look at the top social media networking platforms for businesses and how to use them to achieve business goals in your entrepreneurial journey.

Facebook

Facebook is the obvious choice for business promotion due to their expansive audience. You can create a business page, groups for your business, and even hold events. On Facebook, you can also collect reviews and testimonials, which help increase your authority online.

Set up your Facebook business page profile and include any contact details for potential customers and clients. Create a group for your business that is connected to your business page. Make sure you welcome new group members to your Facebook page with a welcome post under the members' tab in your group. Doing so will tag new group members, making the rest of your business posts more visible in their newsfeed.

Join groups on Facebook for networking in your field if you are a mom and an entrepreneur I recommend starting with Boss Moms. If you want to learn how to funnel massive amounts of ideal customers to your sales page, join the official Click Funnels page.

Instagram

Instagram is a social network that only allows you to post if you have a photo attached. The Gram was acquired by Facebook, which increased their popularity instantly. Most Instagram users are millennials and the younger generation. Your target audience may be here if you are targeting a younger age group.

The jury is still out on whether you should create a business account or personal account for your business on Instagram. If you create a business account, you will gain analytics for your account and have the ability to create ads, but you lose some of the story features of a personal account. Some users who switched from a personal IG account to a business account reported a steep decline in engagement on their Instagram posts.

LinkedIn

With over 575 million users, and 260 million active users per month, LinkedIn is the premier site to network with other entrepreneurs. Through LinkedIn, you can grow your team, spread brand awareness, and grow your social circle with professionals in your industry. Not only will you want to set up a personal account to start networking and building authority, but also set up a business page to expand your reach online.

Make sure to use the featured post section on LI to highlight media related to your business, or anything that increases trust with potential customers.

Pinterest

Does your business have information worth saving, or rather, "pinning?" Pinterest members create boards of information they can reference later. Save images from your company site, information from blog posts, and industry-related imagery to your Pinterest account for instant backlinks to your site.

Join group boards on Pinterest or look into Tailwind Tribes to get your pins saved by people in your niche.

Twitter

The fastest-moving social media network, Twitter posts seem to only stay relevant for a few minutes after you post. If you use the appropriate hashtags, you can extend the life of your tweets and your reach on the platform.

YouTube

Create video explainers about your products and services and share them on the #1 video hosting site in the world. YouTube allows users to follow and subscribe to your channel. Use the platform to announce new launches, spread company news, and tell the world what your company is all about.

Quora

Quora lets users ask questions and answer questions. Based on your expertise, you can become an authority in a specific field. In some cases, Quora will even pay you for your input. Make sure to link your company's website or Facebook Business page to your Quora profile and start answering industry-related questions.

Imgur

Imgur is a platform to upload, share, and browse entertaining images. Crafters and other types of unique businesses do well here when they upload process videos. Show people the inside of your business, share what makes your business unique, and engage with the community. Users can choose to upvote or downvote your images and videos. The more interesting your content, the more likely it will make it to the front page. Imgur has some unspoken rules such as:

- No selfies unless it is Christmas, then selfies are mandatory. Selfies will get you downvoted to oblivion, avoid them at all costs.
- Do not create posts that are meant as ads; create engaging content instead.
- Do not spam the user submission section, if you have many images to share, put them all in one post.

Chapter 8 – Market Your Business

Marketing campaigns are organized, strategized efforts to promote a specific company goal, such as raising awareness of a new product or capturing customer feedback. They typically aim to reach consumers in a variety of ways and involve a combination of media, including but not limited to email, print advertising, television, or radio advertising, pay-per-click, and social media. (Decker 2020)

Having a strong marketing plan is the lifeblood of your business. Create a plan with a clear strategy in mind and know what your end goals are for your marketing campaign. Quantify your results after each campaign to make the next campaign efforts stronger, and keep building a solid marketing plan.

Brand Awareness

Brand awareness is the degree to which customers know about the unmistakable characteristics or pictures of a specific brand of merchandise or administrations. Increasing brand awareness is not just getting a gathering of individuals to remember your brand, but also about building trust and authority.

When they recollect the brand name, however, not what it does, how it can support them, or the worth it offers, at that point, their awareness is just of the name, not the brand.

Utilizing the effect of brand awareness requires your messages to impart what your company does and for what reason that is important to your target customers.

Just with this basic data, will they have the option to connect the brand with that distinction to its incentive during the purchasing decision stage? You want people to remember you when they are ready to make a purchase, and to trust you enough to recommend your company to family and friends.

Promote a New Product or Service

When you have a new product or service launching, it is time to go in to launch mode with your marketing campaign. Try offering customers a preview of the new launch before the general public to generate interest. Use your email list to send a series of launch emails and funnel people in to try your new offer.

Gather Customer Feedback

In order for your business to grow, you need to get feedback from your customers. Whether that feedback is through reviews, surveys, or testimonials, it will be the driving force in improving your business. A campaign for gathering customer feedback can be a survey contest, like you see on the back of a Taco Bell receipt to submit feedback for a chance to win $500. People love getting rewards for their voice being heard, even if it is just a chance to get rewarded.

Boost User Engagement

When your marketing goal is to boost user engagement, you want to post visually stimulating content that gets people talking. Pose questions that relate to your brand while invoking potential customers to respond. Create eye-catching visuals that get people to stop scrolling and respond to your content. Make sure you engage with other accounts, instead of just posting and expecting people to magically engage with your content online.

Set Clear Goals

A marketing campaign without a clear goal will fail to meet any perceived goals. Instead of painting a broad stroke of "increase business," set clear goals for your marketing plan. Do you want to gain 100 email subscribers? Do you want 50 new subscribers? Quantify your goals in a way you can track their success, then restructure your plan if you are not hitting the mark.

Determine How You Will Reach your Audience

To determine how you will reach your audience, we are taking a look at the PESO model, which stands for Paid, Earned, Shared, and Owned types of content and media. Gini Dietrich, the author of Spin Sucks, says, "If you aren't using the PESO model for your communications work, and measuring the meaningful metrics that help an organization grow, you will not have a job in 10 years." (Thabit 2015)

Paid

Paid media is becoming more mainstream for companies by using social media influencers and other forms of paid advertisement. Gone are the days of print ads and commercials dominating the paid media space.

- Print Ads
- Television Ads
- Ads promoted on social media
- Influencer posts

With paid media, you gain analytics to show you how effective your marketing campaign is, allowing you to maximize your reach. (Waddington 2018)

Earned

Earned media comes in the form of press releases and other media sites promoting your company. This can come from pitching third parties such as journalists or influencers who commonly repurpose content. Earned media is typically not paid for, but is beneficial for both the company being promoted, and the company or journalist releasing the media.

- Media Relations
- Blogger Relations
- Organic Influencer Content

Shared

Shared media, also known as social media by some, is content posted on networks such as Twitter, Facebook, and LinkedIn. Messaging platforms such as Snapchat, iMessenger, and WhatsApp can also be hosts for shared content. Shared media can be paid, as in creating ads, or unpaid when posting organic content.

- Facebook
- Twitter
- LinkedIn
- Snapchat
- WhatsApp
- iMessenger

Owned

Owned media is any content that your company has total control over. These can be company-owned apps, your website, and marketing communication collateral. When you invest time and effort into your company's content, it is a highly effective form of distributing company media, and the most cost-effective option. The most effective type of owned media comes from email marketing campaigns stemming from subscribers who have opted in to receive marketing material from your company.

Create a lead magnet or free offer to start building your email list, then start creating your email campaigns targeted at your list of potential clients. Some of the most effective email marketing campaign types are:

- **Welcome email sequences**
- **Abandoned cart coupons**
- **Birthday promotions**
- **Monthly newsletters**

Measuring Marketing Campaigns

The simplest way to measure a marketing campaign is to measure the amount of direct sales revenue the campaign produces. Depending on the goals of your marketing campaign, the sales increase may not be the most important factor for success. If you are looking to increase engagement on social media, check out your analytics for ads and your business page's reach. There are tools built into Facebook and Twitter to measure this information with ease.

If doing an email marketing campaign, measure the number of opens and click-throughs your emails get. Try testing two different emails with your list, and keep the one that performs best.

The main reason you measure results is to improve your marketing campaigns for the future. Without measuring your success, you do not have a benchmark or a way to set clear goals for your business.

Chapter 9 – Do you need to Incorporate or Become an LLC?

When starting out, the short answer to if you need to incorporate or create an LLC is no. However, as you grow, you will need to become an LLC or other type of corporation before making your first hire. One easy way to navigate the time opening your business and forming an LLC is to purchase services from freelancers instead of hiring employees. Read on to learn about your options when incorporating, or choosing not to incorporate your business.

What is an LLC?

A limited liability company (LLC) is a private limited company, specific to the United States. This business model combines factors from a sole proprietorship and a partnership with the limited liability that is allowed corporations. Depending on your state and the type of services you provide, you may be required to form an LLC to conduct business. Forming an LLC protects your personal assets in the event your business goes into debt or gets sued.

What is an S Corp vs. a C Corp?

An S Corp is a pass-through taxable entity, which can have no more than 100 shareholders. Shareholders of S Corporations must be citizens of the United States of America. An S Corp may only have one type of stock. If you plan on selling shares, an S Corp may not be for you.

C Corp is a separate taxable entity. With a C Corp, there is the possibility of double taxation on income that is taxed first on the corporate level, and again when the members of the corporation and shareholders pay personal income taxes. C Corps have an unlimited number of shareholders and no restrictions on ownership based on the citizenship of owners. It is usually easier for a C Corp to obtain funding and equity financing.

What is a Sole Proprietorship?

No formal action needs to be taken to form a sole proprietorship. In a sole proprietorship, you are your business, and taxes are paid on any profit after the loss. You will pay both self-employment and estimated taxes. With a sole proprietorship, you are in complete control of your company and do not have shareholders pulling strings. You will be personally liable if your business is sued, and you will maintain the heavy burden of your business's success or failure. (U.S. Small Business Administration n.d.)

Which one is right for your business?

When deciding how to form your business, check local and state guidelines before making a decision. In some states, you may be required to form an LLC. In others, it is advisable to form an S Corporation. In most cases, you can set up an LLC on your own without hiring an attorney, but forming an S or C Corporation gets a little trickier, and should be done with the help of an attorney.

Chapter 10 – Grow Your Team

If you want to scale your business, you will need a team of dedicated people to help you along the way. That means it is time to start recruiting. Do not just post job ads and hire the first person who applies. Your business is only as strong as those who help you build it.

Decide if you need in-person help or if you are comfortable with your staff working remotely. If you are fine with having remote staff, you can consider hiring freelancers or employing a remote agency to fill your staffing needs.

Create a format for your application process and use an applicant tracking system (ATS) to keep track of candidates as you move them through the recruitment process.

All of the networking you did on LinkedIn will help you fill positions at your new company. Reach out to your network for recommendations when filling high-profile positions such as marketing managers, sales leads, and accountants. Choose people whose work ethic and availability meet your needs.

When creating a job ad, make sure you highlight the benefits of working with your company. As a new business, you will likely receive fewer applicants than your competitors who may even be paying higher wages. Create benefits packages that lure people in to work with you, and treat your people fairly when given the opportunity to increase wages.

Depending on the role you need to fill, or the project you need to be completed, try posting a job ad on one of these online job portals:

- Indeed
- LinkedIn
- GitHub
- Fiverr
- Upwork
- Snagajob
- Monster
- Craigslist

Beyond using portals, you can employ a recruiting firm to help fill roles within your company quickly. A recruiting firm will typically charge between 10 and 20% of the first year's salary to fill an open position. Companies like Reflik help startups and small businesses fill critical roles in their business and have access to thousands of freelance recruiters worldwide. (Team Reflik 2020)

Chapter 11 – Keeping Your Finances in Line

Once you start earning money and making purchases for your business, you will need a way to track that information and keep your finances in line. When starting out, you can use software to assist you, but your best bet is to hire an accountant who specializes in small businesses to keep you out of hot water with both your taxes and your business expenses. The great news is you can often purchase accounting services as a product from a freelancer instead of having to start payroll right away.

You will need to keep track of your profits and losses to avoid paying unnecessary taxes. If you bought a new laptop, track it. If you took a potential client out to dinner, track it. If you bought software to track how much you are spending on your business, track it. My point is, everything needs a record, or else you will end up paying more in taxes than you should. Even worse, you could get audited and not have records available to show the IRS and clear your business, making the audit take even longer. This could result in hefty fines for your business.

Track your inventory, shipping, and any other expenses your business incurs.

Keep track of your receivables, each time you issue an invoice, you record a receivable. In other words, you make a record that a customer owes you money. Once that invoice is paid, the funds should be applied to the invoice, marking the invoice as paid. Without this system, you will lose track of outstanding balances and can end up in the red.

As you track your finances, produce a cash flow statement. This statement will give you a wider understanding of the direction your cash is moving both within your company and externally. You can use bookkeeping software to automatically generate your cash flow statement, saving you time while keeping your finances in line.

When you spend money on your business, keep and log the receipts. Better than saving hundreds of paper receipts, you can scan them and log them in your bookkeeping software. Having a heaping pile of receipts to dig through when figuring out company books will only make things more difficult. Instead of saving a few minutes by not logging each receipt, you are adding days to weeks to your end of quarter reports. Start with an organized system and reap the benefits of preparation.

Keep invoices and receipts logged separately. If you are using a physical filing system, create a file for both receipts and invoices, instead of mixing the two. When receipts and invoices get mixed into the same place, it can become an accounting nightmare. An invoice is a bill sent to a customer, and a receipt is a proof that the transaction happened, given upon receiving payment.

Keep your personal funds separate from those for your business to prevent you from dipping into your business funds for personal purchases. You should also set aside a certain amount for taxes, since you will not have an employer paying your income and estimated taxes automatically. Generally, in the United States, entrepreneurs should put back 30% of their business profits for taxes. The last thing you want is to be surprised with a hefty tax bill you cannot pay, then having to pay fines on top of that for not paying on time.

When it comes to doing taxes for your business, hire a professional who specializes in working with other small to medium-sized businesses. Preparing your taxes on your own may save you money upfront, but getting audited and paying fines will hurt your business. A tax audit can cause you to lose your business license in some cases. It is always best to err on the side of caution when it comes to business taxes. If you are a solopreneur, or sole proprietorship, your taxes will be simpler and can be done by yourself, but a professional can end up saving you money by finding additional credits and tax cuts that you qualify for based on your unique circumstances.

Chapter 12 – Never Stop Learning and Improving your Business

Keep advancing, keep expanding, and keep learning how to make your business grow. The most important step you can take is the first step in starting your business. But, do not let yourself fixate in comfort. You will need to adopt a growth mindset to grow your business. Seek out others you can learn from, find a mentor, and use free and paid education materials that will help you succeed well into the future.

There will be trials and mistakes along the way, remember that no matter what you are learning and you are growing. A growth mindset and adaptability are the keys to success for any business owner in today's world. Remember that at every new step, there will be more research, and you will be more knowledgeable at the end. Try investing in a mentor who has been in your shoes, and take heed in their advice.

Your investment in yourself by reading this book has put you on the path to thriving as a business owner, but do not stop there. Now is your time to shine on and create a new path forward, one where you are in charge of your future.

Disclaimer

Disclaimer: *The information in this book is from my experience in setting up the company that I have owned and operated. There could be unique situations pertaining to your business, where the advice of an attorney is necessary. In these events, consult an attorney at your own discretion. The information in this book is strictly for educational purposes and should not be taken as legal advice. By reading this book, you hold the author, editor, and any ancillary parties as harmless in the event of any legal repercussions.*

References

Brunson, Russell. 2017. *Expert Secrets.* New York: Morgan James Publishing.

Business Dictionary. n.d. *product.* Accessed July 13, 2020.

> http://www.businessdictionary.com/definition/product.html.

—. n.d. *Service Business.* Accessed July 13, 2020. http://www.businessdictionary.com/definition/service-business.html.

Decker, Allie. 2020. *The Ultimate Guide to Marketing Campaigns.* May 09. Accessed July 13, 2020.

> https://blog.hubspot.com/marketing/marketing-campaigns.

Forleo, Marie. 2019. *Everything is Figureoutable: How One Simple Belief Can Help Us Overcome Any Obstacle and Create Unstoppable Success.* New York: Portfolio / Penguin An Imprint of Penguin Random House LLC.

My Biz Starts Here. n.d. *Create Your Business Plan.* Accessed July 13, 2020. https://mybizstartshere.com/plan-your-business/create-your-business-plan/.

Team Reflik. 2020. *Scaling Recruiting Operations with Reflik: InterAction24 Shares Their Experience.* May 28. Accessed July 21, 2020. https://www.reflik.com/blog/scaling-recruiting-operations-with-reflik-interaction24-shares-their-experience/.

Thabit, Mark. 2015. *How PESO Makes Sense in Influencer Marketing.* June 08. Accessed July 20, 2020. https://www.prweek.com/article/1350303/peso-makes-sense-influencer-marketing#:~:text=The%20PESO%20model%2C%20which%20Dietrich,as%20leaders%20within%20their%20industry.

U.S. Small Business Administration. n.d. *Sole Proprietorship.* Accessed July 20, 2020.

> https://www.sba.gov/content/sole-proprietorship.

Waddington, Steven. 2018. *PESO explained for marketing and public relations.* February 14. Accessed July 13, 2020. https://wadds.co.uk/blog/peso-for-marketing-and-pr.

www.ingramcontent.com/pod-product-compliance
Lightning Source LLC
Chambersburg PA
CBHW040245220526
45473CB00001B/371